DIARY OF A MINECRAFT ZOMBIE

BOOK 25

MISSION POSSIBLE

Copyright © 2023 Zack Zombie Publishing

All rights reserved. No part of this publication may be reproduced, distributed, or transmitted in any form or by any means, electronic or mechanical, including photocopying, recording, scanning, or by any information storage or retrieval system, without the prior written permission of the publisher, except in the case of brief quotations embodied in critical reviews and certain other non-commercial uses permitted by copyright law.

This unofficial novel is an original work of fan fiction which is not sanctioned nor approved by the makers of Minecraft. Minecraft is a registered trademark of, and owned by, Mojang Synergies AB, and its respective owners, which do not sponsor, authorize, or endorse this book. All characters, names, places, and other aspects of the game described herein are trademarked and owned by their respective owners. Minecraft ®/TM & © 2009-2022 Mojang.

DIARY OF A MINECRAFT ZOMBIE

BOOK 25

MISSION POSSIBLE

BY
Zack Zombie

MONDAY

'What movie are we gonna watch today?' I asked at dinner.

'Hmmm, it's Dad's turn to pick, so probably some old **PRE-CLASSIC** movie?' Mom replied.

Urgh!

Dad always chooses super lame movies. They were always Pre-Classic movies about stupid quests with really bad special effects or boring stuff about inventions... bad, always bad.

The only movie **WORSE** than Dad's choices was Wesley's pick of General

Underpants and the Invasion of Ocelots. Bleugh!

But no matter how bad the movie was, there was one thing that I still looked forward to...

Favorite movie snack

POPCORN! I liked to rub it in-between the cushions of the couch, to pick up all those tasty **SKIN FLAKES** and dust particles. I always gobbled two full boxes.

Yum!!

That was the best movie EVER! It was called *Operation Beta-RAINS* and it was all about secret agents. Not the boring ones that do all the paperwork, but, like, out in the FIELD! The main guy was Bob Crafter and he had to deliver a **TOP SECRET** package to save the Overworld from being destroyed by the evil Alpha Incorporated. Alpha Incorporated sent a bunch of bad mobs in black suits to stop Bob Crafter from delivering the package. But Bob pulled off the coolest tricks to complete his mission and deliver the package.

Like, there was a scene where Bob walked up the side of a building...

outside! He was using these special suction-shoes, and dangling, like, fifty stories up. It was super awesome!

And then there was an epic scene where Bob was making his getaway in a cool-looking car and being chased by BAD MOBS, and he was throwing stuff back at them and swerving everywhere.

It. Was. Amazing!

How could something Pre-Classic be SO GOOD?

I tried all Bob Crafter's cool parkour and **MARTIAL ARTS** moves in my room after the movie.

But no matter how I jumped or flipped or twisted, it just didn't seem to work. My limbs were all over the room after just rolling onto my bed. Man, how did Bob do all that stuff??

Sigh. I guess being a secret agent can only ever be a dream for me.

I mean, you can't have a super awesome secret agent leaving their body parts all over the place in an epic chase scene.

TUESDAY

'It was just so cool! The way Bob Crafter scaled down the building!' I fanboyed to my friends at school.

'Oh yeah, that's one of my mom's favorite movies,' said Slimey.

'Dude, that scene where Bob crawls through the vents, then lowers himself down with a rope to get the **SECRET ITEM** from the laser-protected room? Dad and I re-watch that scene on zTube all the time,' chimed in Skelee.

'Yeah, and then the final **FACE OFF** with the evil mob? So good,' smiled Creepy.

'Wait... you've all seen it?' I stuttered. 'How could you not tell me about it?!'

All the guys shrugged.

'We thought your parents would've already shown you,' shrugged Skelee.

'And you always say that you hate Pre-Classic movies,' added Creepy.

Skelee, Creepy and Slimey all nodded together.

Oh.

'So do you guys ever think about becoming a **SECRET AGENT** like Bob Crafter?' I asked.

'Yeah!' the guys all answered.

They all showed me their best secret agent moves. Slimey's were definitely the best—he could jump so high he could scale a tall building in no time. Super cool! Although last time he tried this, he was attacked by a Pig and ended up in the mud.

They might look cute but Pigs are the best guards ever

Seeing my friends do such great secret agent moves made me a little sad. I couldn't even do a flip onto my bed without my head rolling off onto the floor.

And it's so hard to put your head back on when the rest of your body can't see it—**REAL UNCO.**

'How was work today, Francis?' asked Mom, while we were eating my favorite dessert: **CAKE!** Good thing Mom wasn't asking me a question. No time to talk: must... eat... cake!

'It was interesting. The new delivery program just started up,' Dad answered through each bite of cake.

'So is that going to be an extra job you need to do?'

'No, they are going to hire some new recruits for the job.'

My ear holes perked up. Delivery? New recruits? That was how Bob Crafter became a secret agent in Operation Beta-RAINS. 'Delivery' was always code—it really meant **'SECRET MISSION'.** Maybe this was my chance to fulfil all my secret agent dreams!

I'd better sneakily extract more information from my source.

'Cough. Cough. Dad, I am interested in this new program the Nuclear Waste Plant just started up. Can you please give me more information?' I asked, using the most grown-up voice and words I knew.

Mom and Dad looked at me. Wesley started laughing.

'What was that, Zombie? Are you feeling a little light-headed?' asked Mom with a very worried look on her face.

'Did a Witch just **POSSESS** my son? Who was that?' Dad laughed, his eyes almost falling out of his eye sockets.

Well... I guess acting like an adult didn't work. My cover was blown.

Was my adult voice THAT bad?

'I was just trying to be **GROWN UP...**' I whispered, trying to hold back the sobs.

'Ah, sorry, Zom Zom. You did really well,' smiled Mom, glaring at Dad.

'Err, yes, very good, son. To, err, answer your question, the Nuclear Waste Plant have a lot of packages they need delivered all the time. So instead of hiring mobs from a delivery company, we are setting up our own delivery program, and we'll need **NEW MOBS** for that,' Dad said.

'Oh yeah? That's cool. How do you apply?' I asked, trying to be casual.

'I think it's online...' Dad answered, but I didn't hear the rest of his answer.

I was already upstairs on my computer, filling out the form to become part of the delivery team at the Nuclear Waste Plant. I'd be a **SECRET AGENT** in no time!

WEDNESDAY

'Anyway, I ended up applying last night.' I was telling the guys about the **DELIVERY PROGRAM** at the Nuclear Waste Plant. 'It was actually really easy.'

I'd taken a screenshot of the form and printed it out to show them.

Full name:	Zackary Julius Zombie
Birthday:	31 October
Address:	16 Brains Road, Mob Village
Contact Z-mail:	zombieizdabest@zmail.com

Interest:	Becoming a secret agent
How did you find out about this job:	My dad works for the Nuclear Waste Plant and he told me.

'I mean, yeah... that's a pretty **EASY** form to fill out,' Skelee agreed.

'I'm pretty sure we had to give more information when we signed up for Creepaway Camp,' muttered Creepy.

'Zombie, are you sure this isn't some dodgy thing? You know your luck with getting mixed up in... uh... funny circumstances,' said a worried Slimey.

I stared at the guys blankly. I didn't know what Slimey was talking about.

I never get caught up in CRAZY SITUATIONS. My life is so boring.

'Nah, it's LEGIT—my dad works there. And I should be alright. What's the worst that can happen?' I replied with a shrug.

Like, really...

The guys looked at each other, then they shrugged, too.

'I can't wait to hear more about this job when you get it,' smiled Creepy.

'Zombie, you've got a **LETTER!**' Mom called as I came through the door after school. 'I left it on the kitchen table.'

I made my way to the kitchen and found a sealed yellow envelope on the table. I decided to take it up to my room to open it.

Sitting down at my desk, I peeled the envelope open and pulled the letter out.

Dear Zackary Zombie,

You have been accepted as part of the delivery team for the Nuclear Waste Plant. Your code name for all future deliveries is 111.

Your first job is to deliver a package to:

28 Petal Way
Sunflower Fields
Forest Biome

The package will be dropped at your current address. Once it arrives, you have no more than five days to deliver the package safely to the specified location.

Best of luck,

The Delivery Program Manager at the Nuclear Waste Plant.

P.S. This letter will explode five minutes after opening to prevent littering. Please make sure the letter is safely secured in a fireproof space.

Wait, five minutes?! When did I open the letter? And how long had I spent reading it? I know Ms. Bones always says my reading is slow, but how slow is slow—

BOOM!

I guess that was five minutes.

It took me another half an hour to put out the fire that had engulfed my desk and was trying to spread across the room. I managed to avoid being respawned, but I needed a new pair of hands from Mom's supply in the basement.

Man, this delivery job seemed to be completely crazy... crazy real, just like in *Operation Beta-RAINS*.

Yeah, the Delivery Program Manager was definitely the head of a team of secret agents and this package delivery job was really a secret agent mission.

Wait, so does that make me...

A SUPER-SECRET AGENT!?

THURSDAY

'Ms. Bones, I'm going on a holiday tomorrow,' I said to my teacher at roll call.

'Where are you going to?'

'Um, just to the Forest Biome. Here's the letter from my parents,' I said, handing her a letter.

This had better work. I was really nervous, so the letter was drenched in **SWEAT**. Mom always tells me a serious letter should be slimy and the slimier the letter, the more seriously it would be taken.

Ms. Bones was squinting as she read the letter. 'Okay, Zombie, it looks fine. Well, what I can read of it anyway. Where were you keeping it? The ink has run so much,' Ms. Bones finally said.

PRRRRRRFFFFTTTTTTT.

'Ewww, what's that smell?!' cried one of the Ghasts in my class.

'It's like **ROTTEN EGGS** that sat in the sun for a week...' gasped a Slime in-between breaths.

What's wrong with a bit of rotten egg?

Then the Skeleton behind me fainted.

I did feel bad for letting one rip. But man, that nervous **FART** was such a good one. I can see why Creepers do it all the time—it's really relaxing.

'WOAH! SO YOU ACTUALLY GOT THE JOB?' shouted the guys when I told them at lunchtime.

'Yup, and I got my **FIRST MISSION** already,' I answered proudly.

'Wait... does that mean you aren't really going on holiday to the Forest Biome with your family? You lied to Ms. Bones?' Skelee asked.

'Zombie, you can't do that!' Creepy shout-whispered, starting to hiss.

I patted my friend on the back, and passed him his Liquid Nitrogen Inhaler. 'Yeah... but it'll be fine. I'm sure Mom and Dad will understand why I did it.'

'It is pretty cool that you get to live your secret agent dream,' sighed Slimey.

'Right?! The message even came in an **EXPLODING ENVELOPE,**' I said proudly.

You're looking at a real secret agent

'Woahhh...' gasped the guys.

'Have you got your secret agent kit ready?' asked Skelee.

'No...'

'DUDE! The package could show up anytime! You have to have your pack ready,' Slimey advised.

'Yeah. Zombie, you don't want to have to jump off a building without a **GRAPPLING HOOK**,' nodded Creepy.

The guys were right... I had to be prepared.

I mean, if I had to jump off a building without a grappling hook, Mom would definitely have enough **EXTRA**

BODY PARTS to fix me up if I just kept my head safe... but I'd probably crush the package.

I'd better get packing.

Once I finished dinner, I went upstairs to pack for my mission.

Like any good secret agent, I made a list of everything that I would need:

- ☒ Grappling hook
- ☒ Heat-signature glasses
- ☒ Spy hearing amplifier device
- ☒ Defense weapon (a Golden Sword would be AWESOME)

- ☒ Long distance telescope lenses

- ☒ Night-vision goggles.

After coming up with this list, I went up to the **ATTIC**. I remembered my dad saying that my great-great-great-great-great-great-great-great-great-great-grandfather (that's ten greats!) was a secret agent for the Nether Army during the Great Biome War in the early Pre-Classic era. I figured I might be lucky and find some really old-fashioned **SPY GEAR**.

But after searching for what seemed like hours, I couldn't find anything that looked anything like secret agent stuff.

So I snuck into Wesley's toy box. In the end, I found some of Wesley's toys that kind of did the job:

- Fishing hook with string
- 3D glasses from an activity book
- Stethoscope from an old doctor dress-up outfit
- Water pistol (my plan was to make it squirt **SPICY SAUCE** instead... that would really burn)
- A telescope that had cool beads in the lens (yeah, it didn't help me see but it did look cool)
- A torch.

I found my **BACKPACK** and stuffed all my secret agent gear into it.

Kinda surprised it all fits...

I was just finishing zipping up my bag, when—

DING, DONG.

'Who can it be? It's so late,' I heard Mom say tiredly, as she lumbered towards the door.

'Don't worry, Mom, it's uh... just... Skelee... dropping off some homework!' I yelled, rushing for the door.

It must be the package, and I couldn't have Mom knowing about my super-secret mission!

When I opened the door, the **PACKAGE** was on the doorstep.

Cleverly disguised as an ordinary package

Ah, I was sooo excited! My mission had begun! And although I was really curious about what was in the box, I resisted opening it. **FIRST RULE** of being a secret agent: never open the top secret package you are delivering to complete the mission.

FRIDAY

'Mom, I think I'm getting sick—*cough, cough, cough*,' I said, clearing my throat.

'Oh sweetie, you were fine yesterday. Let me check your forehead,' Mom sighed.

Good thing I knew she was gonna do that. I'd used a **HAIRDRYER** on my forehead to make it feel like I had a temperature.

Although, I think I held it there too long—my forehead got so hot it started peeling. I wouldn't be doing that again.

'Oh my goodness, Zombie, you're burning up!' Mom cried. 'I should take you to the doctor! Let me call Rhonda to say I can't have lunch with her and cancel my **POO-GA** class, and we'll go straight to the doctor after we drop off Wesley at Pre-Scare School.'

'No, no! It's alright, Mom. It's not that bad, I'll just, uh... sleep it off,' I answered.

'Oh, I don't know, Zombie...' Mom said, unconvinced.

'Really, Mom, it's probably just a cold. I'll go straight back to bed.'

'Hmmm, okay. Just don't let me catch you playing **VIDEO GAMES** when I get back,' Mom said suspiciously, and she went back to getting breakfast ready.

Phew! So glad Mom believed I was sick... I didn't have time for school, I had to work out how to deliver this package.

Once the house was empty, I turned my computer on and started looking at how I was gonna get to Sunflower Fields.

I did a quick **ZOOGLE** search and I didn't realize how far away the Forest Biome was! If I walked, it would take 187 hours... that's over a week!

I don't remember it being this far away ↙

Yeah, that was a huge 'NOPE' from me.

So I started looking at buses, sleeper Minecart trains and even flying and **AUTOMATIC MINECART ITEM TRANSPORT SYSTEMS.** There was no way I'd be able to build an Automatic Minecart

Item Transport System, even with Steve's help. So flying was definitely going to be the fastest way to get there, but there was no way I could afford it with my pocket money.

But if I borrowed Dad's Credit Card when he got home from work...

Nah, I shouldn't do that. It would be too easy to track down my movements. **SECOND RULE** of being a secret agent: never leave a trail for any mob to follow you.

'Zombie, did you use Dad's Credit Card to go shopping on Zbay?' Mom called out, sounding angry.

Uh oh.

I slowly crept down the stairs. Peering around the doorframe into the kitchen, I saw the package Mom was talking about, sitting on the table.

'No, I was—cough, cough—sleeping all day,' I replied in my best sick voice.

I HAD spent most of my day on Zbay, but not buying stuff. I was trying to sell everything in my room. It was all part of my GENIUS plan to make some quick money.

But I hadn't had much luck so far. I don't know why my **BOOGER SCULPTURE** of the Ocean Monument hadn't already sold... I mean, at only 100,000 Coins, it was a total bargain.

So I had no idea what this package was. Then I saw the 'TOP SECRET' stamp on the side... it must be another delivery mission!

Another mission already?

'Oh... um... it must be a gift from... Steve! He's been on an adventure in the... Ocean Biome,' I fibbed. Was it really lying if my fingers were knotted behind my back?

'Right... well, that's nice of him. Aren't you going to open it then?' asked Mom.

'Uh... I'll open it in my room. Steve likes playing **TRICKS**,' I replied as I grabbed the package and ran up to my room before Mom could ask me any more questions.

Carefully cutting open the parcel, I found a bag and a letter inside.

This time, I took the letter to the **BATHROOM** to read it:

Dear 111,

Please find inside everything you need to safely deliver the package:

- Airplane tickets

- Sleeper Minecart train tickets

- Snacks.

Best of luck on your delivery!

The Delivery Program Manager at the Nuclear Waste Plant.

P.S. Like the last letter, this one will also explode five minutes after opening. Please make sure the letter is safely secured in a fireproof space.

Yes, travel problem solved! Now I didn't have to sell my booger collection!

I quickly threw the letter into the toilet and flushed it away. There, a totally safe and secure fireproof space.

I went back to my room, pretty proud of how I'd solved all my problems.

BOOM!

'Ahhhh! Why is it raining in the kitchen?!' I heard Mom yell from downstairs.

OOPS.

'That was Steve's trick,' I yelled back, quickly shutting my bedroom door.

SATURDAY
6:45

BZZZT. BZZZT.

Man, why did the Nuclear Waste Plant book such an early plane ticket?

I'd picked out my clothes before I went to bed, and I'd decided not to wear my usual purple and turquoise combo. Inspired by Bob Crafter's outfit choices in *Operation Beta-RAINS*, I'd laid out an **ALL-BLACK** outfit.

I got ready as quickly as I could. I even **DIRTIED** my teeth! I had to look my best for my first mission!

Taking a quick look at my alarm clock, I could see that I had a few minutes to spare. So I quickly posed in front of the mirror for a selfie.

Man, I really looked like a secret agent. Black is definitely my color.

But selfies are hard when you have no fingers. Urgh!

Mission ready!

Before I headed out the door, I decided to write a note to my parents. I thought about lying and saying I was staying with Steve, but I was a **BRAVE** secret agent now. I should probably be honest about why I would be away for the weekend.

Hey family,

I actually applied for that delivery program at the Nuclear Waste Plant, and they offered me a job. I have a package to deliver to Sunflower Fields in the Forest Biome. I should be back in time for school next week.

Have a great weekend without your favorite son! (Just joking, Wesley!)

Z

I left it on the kitchen table and raced out the door. Gotta catch that bus or I'll miss my flight!

I'd never been to a scareport before... and wow, it was a crazy place! I mean, it was so early but it looked like the whole Biome was there. There were mobs everywhere! A lot of them pulled suitcases that looked big enough to fit a full-grown Ocelot inside. What were they all carrying?

The scareport also had a really weird smell. It was so... clean. Like, where was the comforting smell of old farts, mold and **SWEATY CLOTHES?**

I had no idea what to do, so I watched what everyone else was doing. They were taking their tickets to a mob with a fancy little scarf around her neck. Grabbing my ticket out of my backpack, I lined up at the counter. Luckily the line wasn't that long. Waiting was sooo **BORING!**

'Next, please,' a mob called out from the counter.

I went up and handed my ticket to the mob and she began to tap away at her computer.

'Are you travelling alone?' she asked, looking at me suspiciously.

Eek, she was going to blow my cover! 'Yes, I am very grown-up and always travel alone,' I bluffed.

She frowned, but went back to tapping on her computer.

And then from the corner of my **EYE SOCKET,** I saw some mobs in black suits shuffling around the scareport scanner everyone was walking through to get to the planes. They were whispering to each other.

Pretty clever way to check people for unauthorized snacks before they board the planes

My secret agent senses told me something was **DEFINITELY OFF** about them.

I quickly turned back to look at the mob behind the counter.

What if they were after the package? They'd stop at nothing to get it, that's for sure.

Maybe I could go around the scanner and avoid them. I checked under my arm quickly... nah, there were security officers lined up on either side of the scanner. I'd have to go through it if I wanted to board the plane. And I had to board the plane—I couldn't fail this early on in my mission!

I had to think of a way to quickly get the package and me safely through... but how?

Think, **PEA-SIZED BRAIN,** think! Figure out what to do!

As the mob at the counter handed back my ticket, I saw another massive suitcase roll by with a sticker saying **'FOREST BIOME'.** A suitcase that was big enough to fit a teenage Zombie...

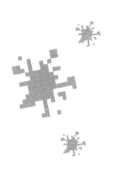

SATURDAY, LATER

It had been a while since I'd snuck into that mob's suitcase.

I'd managed to **SQUEEZE** in when they stopped to talk to someone in the huge queue for the scanner. Man, it was hard though. Lucky I can go to pieces! I had to make sure my legs went in before my body, and then my head last. And I had to be quick!

But it worked. We'd gone through the scanner without being stopped, so I was able to avoid being captured by the evil mobs in black suits. I thought about getting out after that, and boarding the plane properly. But I figured that if they knew I'd be at the scareport, they probably also knew which flight I was supposed to take. So I stayed in the **SUITCASE.** That way, they wouldn't find me and I'd still get onto the flight to the Forest Biome.

Genius pea-sized brain at work!

Although I did doubt myself for a little bit. Especially since I accidentally put my nose next to my butt.

I totally get why the Skeleton fainted in my class the other day.

It was also such a bumpy ride. It reminded me of a **ROLLER COASTER** at the Great Minecraft Adventure Forest Biome theme park.

But it had really calmed down now. So, it should be safe to come out... right?

I took the chance and opened the zip. My legs rolled out before I could catch them, but I managed to put my head back on my body alright. It was pretty dark, and I couldn't see my legs anywhere, but I'd packed the **TORCH** in my backpack for situations just like this one.

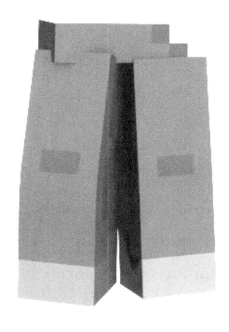

Oh legs, where are you?

It took a while but I finally found my legs in a corner, hidden by a bunch of other suitcases. It felt good to be whole again!

And when I saw the other suitcases it gave me an idea. The evil mobs in black suits might have seen me in my black clothes at the scareport check-in... I needed to come up with a new outfit to blend into the crowd when we landed.

So, I opened a few suitcases to give myself some **DISGUISE** options. Hopefully their owners wouldn't mind. I picked suitcases that were my favorite colors: turquoise and purple.

But all the suitcases I opened must have been owned by girl mobs. The clothes all had flowers and cats and stuff on them.

At first I was **GROSSED OUT,** but then I realized that might work better for my disguise. The bad mobs were gonna be looking for a teen Zombie boy... not a teen Zombie girl!

So I picked out a skirt and a big hat with a bow, and stowed them in my backpack. I also picked out a hair ribbon and a glittery T-shirt with a cat on it to put on now.

Disguise one!

Yup, it's the **PERFECT** disguise. I packed my black outfit into my backpack too. My bag was getting quite full...

After repacking the suitcases I'd opened, I was pretty tired. I had no idea what the time was or how long the flight was supposed to be… but it felt like it was bedtime.

THIRD RULE of being a secret agent: grab your sleep whenever you can, cause you might not get another chance. Man, Bob Crafter taught me so much in *Operation Beta-RAINS*.

SATURDAY...
LATER AGAIN

THUNK!

AHHHH! What was that?

I opened my eyes to complete darkness. Where was I? Did I oversleep?

THUNK, THUNK!

After the **THUNKS**, I remembered where I was.

I was a secret agent inside a suitcase, hiding from evil mobs in black suits, delivering a package to Sunflower Fields in the Forest Biome.

Woah... how did I get to be so cool?

THUNK, THUNK!

Man, the plane must be landing soon, because I could feel my **STOMACH DROP.**

Like, literally. Pretty sure my stomach was outside of my body!

After a bit of a bumpy landing, the plane rolled to a stop. I was pretty proud I didn't vomit throughout the landing process.

But that was when I had a thought... what if the bad mobs were waiting for their own luggage at the carousel?

I couldn't risk it. I'd need to **BAIL OUT** before the owner of this suitcase collected it anyway.

I opened the zipper a little so I could see what was happening. A Zombie Pigman and an Iron Golem were pulling suitcases out of the plane and tossing them onto Minecarts. Eventually, they made it to the suitcase I was hiding in.

'Oooffft, Barry, mind giving me some help? This is a heavy one,' came a voice outside my suitcase as it started moving.

I couldn't see much, but I felt the suitcase being lifted. Then it fell with a large THUD onto what must have been a pile of other suitcases.

I'll definitely have **BRUISES** tomorrow.

'Man, what did this guy pack in his suitcase?' came another voice.

'Maybe it belongs to an Enderman, and it's packed full of **ENDER PEARLS** to sell at the market?' suggested the first voice.

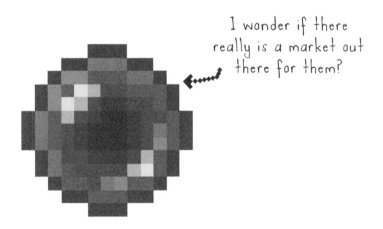

I wonder if there really is a market out there for them?

There was a sudden WHIR and I could feel the suitcase start to move... I must have been thrown onto a Minecart.

I peeked out of the suitcase again. The mob driving the Minecart had his back towards the suitcases and was paying no attention to what was happening behind him. I realized this was my chance to **ESCAPE!**

So I fully opened the suitcase and stuck myself back together. Then I jumped from the Minecart. I didn't manage to do a cool roll onto the tarmac, like the time Bob Crafter jumped out of a moving car and landed on his feet. Instead, I landed in pieces.

Man, if there was a competition for Zombie teens to put themselves back together, I am pretty certain that I would get **FIRST PLACE,** what with all the practice I was getting.

SUNDAY
5:26

GRRRR.

I quickly clutch my tummy. I hadn't eaten anything since Friday night and I'd even skipped dessert to get ready for this mission.

Man, I'd been so looking forward to trying airplane food. From what I've heard, airplane food is very mushy and looks like globs of an **UNKNOWN BROWN SUBSTANCE.**

Yum!

The more I thought about food, the **HUNGRIER** I got, so I just put all my energy into walking. And it felt like I had been walking forever.

After rolling onto the tarmac, I'd started walking towards the closest Forest Biome town. I had a ticket for the Minecart train to take me from there to Sunflower Fields. I was meant to catch a bus from the scareport to the station, but it was too big of a risk with those evil mobs lurking around.

But I must have made a mistake in guessing how far away the village was from the scareport. I mean, it was only a finger-width away from the scareport on the map, but I'd been walking for hours!

Maps aren't easy to read...

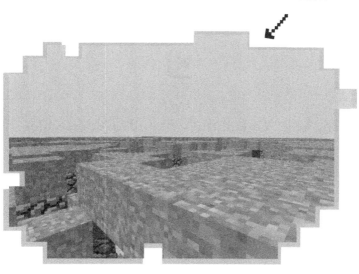

My steps slowed as my tummy grumbled more and more. I saw my life FLASH before my eyes: memories of me and Wesley playing, of hanging out with Creepy, Slimey and Skelee, and going on adventures with my best mate, Steve.

I had a good thirteen years of **UNDEAD** life, didn't I?

'Hey, kid. You okay?' asked a deep voice.

I slowly opened my eye sockets to see an older Creeper in a Nuclear Waste Plant uniform. He was leaning over, nudging me gently with his foot.

'Have I **RESPAWNED?** Is this the next life? Are you an angel, sir?' I asked.

'Uh, no. You're still in the Overworld. Why are you lying on the ground?'

'Oh. I thought I re-died of hunger,' I muttered, and my tummy grumbled in response.

'Woah, that's quite the loudest roar I've heard. And I've been to The Nether,' replied the old Creeper. 'Let's get you something to eat.'

I know Mom taught me never to get into a stranger's car, but I was sooo tired! And this mob worked for the Nuclear Waste Plant, so he was basically a friend. I mean, we worked for the same company.

He drove me to a **DROOL AND GRUEL** diner and he ordered me some food. When the food came, I did nothing but gobble it.

I don't even know what I ate. Maybe all the knocking around in the plane had ruined the last of my taste buds.

'You don't happen to be a delivery mob for the Nuclear Waste Plant, do you?' asked the Creeper.

I nearly choked. 'Cough. Cough.'

'I'll take that as a yes.'

'Er... Cough. Cough.'

'Well, good thing I bumped into you. I helped develop the delivery program,' smirked the Creeper. 'Name's Kabooms Fitzgerald, but you can just call me DR FITZ.'

My savior!

'Herlllooo,' I managed to say, my mouth **STUFFED** with food. Mom would be so proud of my good manners.

'So, kid. From my understanding, the package is actually missing a component and needs to be recalled before it can be delivered to the recipient at Sunflower Fields.'

Huh?

'Um... in simpler terms, you need to grab another item before you can make the delivery.'

Oh!

'Yeah, the packing team forgot to wait for this part to arrive before sending it to you. So, you just need to go to the Redstone Inc. building to collect it. Go to the front desk and show them this card and they should let you up to **LEVEL 57** with no problems,' explained Dr. Fitz, as he handed me a card with all the details on it. 'The building is right around the corner so I'm happy to give you a ride there.'

He was about to get up when I felt a shiver along my spine. Normally, I would think it was just a **WORM** enjoying the dirty shirt I was wearing, but I wasn't wearing my dirty shirt. It must be my secret agent instincts kicking in. Something was definitely up.

Then I heard something WHHHHRRRRRR past my earholes.

SUNDAY
6:43

Luckily, I was able to dodge the cup that was thrown at me. Well, it was more like my head fell off as I moved it too quickly. But still counts!

Dr. Fitz wasn't as lucky and the cup hit him square in the head. He started **HISSING**... Man, I hope he had his Liquid Nitrogen Inhaler on him. My head was rolling across the ground and as it spun, I saw mobs in black suits burst through the diner's front door. How'd they find me again?! I had to find my head... quick!

After all the piecing back together of my body lately, I was able to get a hold of myself pretty quickly. My body grabbed my backpack and the card Dr. Fitz had passed to me, scooped up my head and **BOLTED** out of there.

It was the package in my backpack they wanted, so if I wasn't there they should just leave Dr. Fitz alone.

I ran as fast as I could, but the evil mobs were gaining on me.

That was when I remembered my chili sauce-filled water pistol!

I'd filled Wesley's water pistol with the chili sauce my dad said almost re-killed him. He and his friends like to do chili-eating **COMPETITIONS** and when they ate this sauce... well, let's just say that some of his friends were respawned.

It's not called Ghost Pepper Chili Sauce for nothing!

Dad got to take the bottle home because he was the only one that survived.

Anyway, I could hear the mobs in black suits getting closer and closer. Their shoes weren't the quietest... they had clicky boots that were louder than the heels some of the teachers wear to school.

I waited until the **CLICKITY-CLACKITY** of their heels got right up close behind me, then twisted my arms around and shot the chili sauce right into the mob's eye!

'AHHHHHHHHH!!!' cried the evil mob as he dropped to the ground and curled up clutching his eyes. The second evil mob tripped over the first, and landed on top of him.

Man, that CHILI **SAUCE** worked even better than I thought it would! I managed to escape the mobs chasing me, and found a spot down a dark alley to stop and catch my breath... I'd have to ask Mom to get me a new pair of lungs when this was all over.

It took a while before I felt ready to go back out into the world. But I pulled myself together. I needed to complete my mission. There was a mob waiting in Sunflower Fields for this package to be delivered! And they'd need the whole package, so I had to get that last part!

Now, to find the **REDSTONE INC.** building that was just around the corner...

But which corner?

I wish I'd paid more attention to the map-reading lessons in Scare School... maps are hard! I'd tried all the 'just-around-the-corners' I could see on the map and it was not working.

I finally sat on a park bench to try and re-gather my thoughts. There weren't that many to gather, what with my pea-sized brain.

I wondered if it was possible to get a **PRUNE-SIZED BRAIN** instead... the extra muscles might help me remember how to read maps properly. I'd have to ask Mom if the **MORGUE** stocked them...

It was time to face facts. Maybe this delivery job was just too much for a teenage Zombie? Maybe Zombies were not made to be secret agents?

Sigh.

I looked up and saw a bright red light. It was pretty high up, so I plucked out my eyeball and pointed it towards the light to see what it was...

Could it be?

WHAT IN THE OVERWORLD?

I found it!

I managed to find the building! Now to get there...

SUNDAY
8:15

After trying many more 'just-around-the-corners', I somehow made it to the Redstone Inc. building. Oh man, it was **GINORMOUS!** I didn't know so much glass existed in the whole Overworld.

Some mobs were already heading into work, even though it was Sunday, and I got a few weird looks as I followed them inside. I guess it wasn't everyday they saw a teenage Zombie wearing... wait, I was still wearing that Cat T-shirt! How embarrassing!

Running into the closest bathroom, I changed back into my much cooler, all-black secret agent outfit. When I came out again, I still got stares from the adult mobs, but definitely less. At least **10%** less.

Since I had to show the card that Dr Fitz gave me, I walked towards the main desk in the center of the open floor. But then I saw a very serious-looking group of mobs.

And they all happened to be wearing **BLACK SUITS...**

I ducked behind a pillar. Man, why didn't these evil mobs just leave me alone?

Now I had to find another way up to Level 57...

So glad I watched *Operation Beta-RAINS*. In the few seconds I had to make a decision about where to go to avoid the bad mobs, I remembered Bob Crafter crawling silently through the air vents. So I ran through the fire exit door, pulled the grill out of the wall and climbed into the vent.

Wait...

I probably could've just used the stairs in the fire exit to get to Level 57.

Urgh! Pea-sized brain!

Oh, well. The vent method was much cooler anyway.

I had perfected what I called the **VENT SHUFFLE.** It was all about moving your hips in the right way and then shuffling your elbows and shoulders in rhythm. Good thing they made us learn how to **SALSA DANCE** last year in Scare School.

Who knew salsa was great secret agent practice?!

But then I remembered I still had to get up to Level 57 somehow... I couldn't crawl backwards to the stairs, which meant I had to find my way to the elevator shaft.

Hearing the whirring of heavy metal wires, I shuffled my way towards the sound. I finally came to an opening and stuck my head out.

BZZZZTT.

Luckily, I pulled my head back at just the right time to avoid losing it when the elevator went past. In *Operation Beta-RAINS*, Bob waited for the elevator to come up from the bottom of the building and then he jumped on the top of the elevator, rode it up and jumped back into the vents on the level he wanted... seemed easy enough.

That was when I heard the elevator come back up.

3.

2.

1.

JUMP!

Okay. That wasn't as easy as Bob Crafter made it out to be.

I had to try three more times before I was able to successfully get all of me onto the top of the elevator.

My bag made the first jump, my legs the second jump and then, finally, my body joined the rest of me. How did Bob do it? Maybe being a **REAL-LIFE** secret agent just wasn't as amazing as it looked?

Anyway, it took me another four rides of the elevator going up and down before I was able to jump into the right vent for Level 57. I had to really focus to get my bag and me into the right vent at the right time.

But once I was inside the vent, I was **BACK IN BUSINESS.**

I vent-shuffled my way around, trying to figure out where the missing item that I needed was. I didn't have a map of the building to figure out where the rooms were... not that a map would've helped me since I didn't even know what room it was in.

Luckily, it seemed like the vent only led to one opening. And it was an opening into a room that seemed to protect a **SUPER-SECRET** item sitting on a stand in the middle.

It was a very white room and there were red laser beams everywhere. It basically screamed, 'I AM A SUPER-SECRET ITEM.'

Obviously the secret Item I need

I looked closer and could see that the item had some string tied around it.

Good thing I packed my secret agent kit. I took out the fishing hook and string, looped them together and lowered the hook out through the vent grill towards the package. Nearly there... but then the hook stopped about half a meter above the package. The string wasn't long enough!

Now what? I racked my pea-sized brain.

Then I had a **BRAIN-WAVE!** I got out the Cat T-shirt and looked at it. If I ripped it into one long piece and tied that around myself, I could drop myself out of the vent, just like Bob Crafter in *Operation Beta-RAINS*.

I wouldn't set the laser alarms off, because I'd be hanging from the ceiling, but I'd be able to get the string and hook closer to the package so I could catch the package.

I was a **GENIUS!**

I pulled the grill up to let me through. Carefully, I ripped the T-shirt, tied it around my waist and tucked the end underneath the grill. Once I was sure it was stuck fast, I lowered myself out of the vent and down towards the package. Then I started **FISHING** for the package.

And somehow, it worked! With me dangling from the tied-up T-shirt, the piece of string was just long enough for the fishing hook to grab onto the string around the package.

Slowly, I pulled the item up.

CREAK. CREAK.

I froze, then twisted my head and saw the vent grill had slid backwards and was now hanging across the opening, with the end of the T-shirt caught between the **SHARP EDGES**.

RIIIIIPPP.

The T-shirt was tearing apart.

It was then that I realized I could have stayed in the vent and tied the T-shirt to the end of the string to make it longer, without dangling myself from the ceiling. Duh!

RIIIIPPP!

UH OH.

☀ SUNDAY ☀
9:29

BRRRPP. BRRRP. BRRRRRP.

'DANGER. INTRUDER ALERT.'

The alarm went off as I fell through the **LASER BEAMS.**

BRRRPP. BRRRP. BRRRRRP.

'DANGER. INTRUDER ALERT.'

Oh man. I'd been so close to perfectly executing a recovery mission just like Bob Crafter. So close!!

But I'd have plenty of time to worry about that later. Right now, I needed to move. I picked up my fallen backpack and shoved the new package in there as well. Then I made the quickest outfit change in the history of **ACTION MOVIES...**

I coolly strolled down the hallway and caught the elevator, pretending like I was supposed to be there. Really, I was so nervous that my sweat created a pool around my feet on the elevator floor. I sneakily used my backpack to wipe the pool of sweat up. Luckily, no mob entered the lift as it went down to the ground floor.

Just as I expected, the **EVIL MOBS** in black suits were standing in front of me as the elevator door opened. Good thing I changed my outfit.

Meet Zombi-rella

The bad mobs were expecting a teen Zombie boy wearing black... not a

TEEN ZOMBIE GIRL! They just walked into the elevator as I walked out. I was definitely getting the hang of the disguise part of this secret agent job.

I gave a huge sigh of relief as I walked out of the Redstone Inc. building. Now I could finish the delivery. And this last part should be the easiest bit. I mean, all I had to do was sit on a Minecart train…

When I get home after this mission, I am definitely going to ask Dad to teach me how to read a map. I'd been walking round and round, trying to find the Minecart train station.

Finally, I asked an adult mob where the station was in my sweetest, high-pitched Zombie girl voice. She replied, 'Oh sweetie, it's just around the corner.'

Urgh! That answer has become my **WORST DAYMARE...**

It took me forever to find—it was NOT 'just around the corner'!

Not only was the station hard to find... but then the specific platform the train to Sunflower Fields was on was **IMPOSSIBLE** to find. Why would any place need more than six platforms? And this station had to have nearly thirty... crazy!

I found the right one just as the train was about to leave. As the whistle blew, I managed to jump into the last Minecart carriage.

I made it! Although, my backpack did get stuck as the door closed, so I had to stand right up against the door until the next stop.

But my **HAT** was fine...

I really like this hat...

✷ SUNDAY ✷
10:59

The train had emptied after three or four stops, so I managed to get a spot to sit. My legs were very happy to rest after all that shuffling and racing around.

I hadn't sat since chowing down that food with Dr Fitz...

I hope he didn't **COMBUST.** He seemed like a good dude. I tried watching the hills roll by for a while, but I got bored real quick. I opened my pack and rummaged around, but I'd already eaten all the snacks the

Nuclear Waste Plant had given me. I started poking at the package from Redstone Inc.

Man, I wonder how Bob Crafter resisted opening the secret packages he had to deliver? I had to keep **SLAPPING** my hand away so I didn't open them. One slap was so hard, my hand flew off into an old Slime's head.

It was so embarrassing having to go up and ask for my hand back... and then having to dig into their head to get it back out.

SORRRRYYYYYY!

After that, I was suddenly very tired and decided to take a nap.

'Next stop, Sunflower Fields,' came the train announcer's voice.

ACK!

I jolted awake and looked around. There was only a handful of mobs left on the train. I quickly tucked the packages back in my backpack. Putting my hat on my head, I got up and waited for the door to open.

The train rolled into the station and from the window, I caught a glimpse of **BLACK SUITS...**

☀ SUNDAY ☀
12:16

Man, not them again!!

I fixed the hat to sit lower, so my face was blocked from the evil mobs in black suits. Then I stood tall and walked very elegantly out of the Minecart carriage and onto the platform. Exactly how **ZOMBI-RELLA** would walk... not at all how Zombie would walk.

The bad mobs didn't even notice me! It was definitely the hat and elegant walk.

I started to relax. But just as I thought I'd made it out of the station safely, I heard a yell behind me and then the clickity-clackity of heels.

I twisted my head back to look and, yup, the mobs in black suits were **CHASING** me. They must have remembered my hat from the elevator in the Redstone Inc. building.

Running as fast as my very tired feet could take me, I slid between two walls. It was time for another outfit change. I was happy to get rid of the skirt but the hat...

It was hard... but I threw the hat away, too.

So long,
my friend

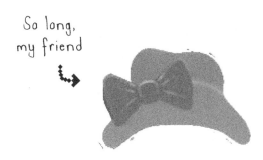

After giving my hat a proper farewell, I changed back into my **AWESOME,** all-black secret agent outfit. Peering around the walls, I looked to see if there were any other mobs in black suits waiting for me. The coast looked clear, so I stepped back out into the street.

I was meant to catch a bus to take me the last little way to Petal Way...

But, of course, the mobs in black suits were waiting for me at the bus stop.

I'd have to come up with another way to get the package to the correct house. And I was NOT walking.

Quickly scanning my surroundings, I saw some **BIKES**... and one didn't have a chain lock.

Grabbing my pen out of my backpack, I left a note:

> Borrowing your bike. Being chased by bad guys. Will get it back to you... somehow. Thanks.

My legs felt like they were about to **FALL OFF**...

Who knew that bike-riding could make you so tired?

There were just so many hills...

After what felt like ten years (seriously, it felt like I lived more than half my life over again cycling up those **CRAZY** hills!), I finally made it to Petal Way.

Now I just had to find number 28...

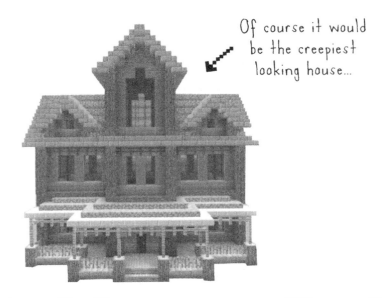

Of course it would be the creepiest looking house...

The driveway for number 28 was up a very steep hill, so I stashed the bike and started hiking to the top.

Man, I have never worked my poor legs so hard in all my thirteen years. My legs were going to look so toned! Well, as toned as undead legs could be, anyway.

After what seemed like climbing up a trillion stairs, I used the last bit of my energy to knock on the front door of the house.

MISSION ACCOMPLISHED!!

This must be how Bob Crafter felt every time he finished a mission. Man, it was such a good feeling.

I got the packages out of my bag ready.

From inside, I could hear footsteps approaching the door. I wondered who the **MYSTERIOUS** mob receiving the package would be...

Wait, was that a clickity-clackity in the mob's step?

CRIIIK.

☀ SUNDAY ☀
1:46

'AGAIN?!' I shouted as a mob in a black suit opened the door.

I ditched them back at the station. How did they beat me here?!

'Oh man, you have been a **TRICKY** one to catch,' sighed the Enderman that opened the door. There was a Blaze in a black suit floating behind him.

How was that suit even staying on the Blaze? Why hadn't it burned? Was it an **ENCHANTED** suit?

Woah...

That thought took me 1.7 seconds, then I realized I had to run. The evil mobs in black suits were NOT going to stop me from completing my mission when I was finally at the finish line!

But how did they know where the package was supposed to be delivered? And how did they get inside?

These questions were flying through my pea-sized brain as I spun around to run...

But before I could take a single step, the Blaze in the black suit floated to block my path of escape.

'Ah, no way. You're not getting away from us this time, dude,' shouted the Blaze, starting to burn up.

'Get away from me! You can't stop me from completing my mission...' I shouted.

'**MISSION?**' asked the Enderman.

'Nah, dude. We're not here to stop you from delivering your package,' seethed the Blaze. 'We are here to stop you from delivering your package to the wrong address.'

Huh?

'What?' I asked the two mobs, clutching the packages close to my chest.

'**111**, we're here to give you an update on your delivery instructions,' said the Enderman.

Huh? Why would the evil mobs want to give me an update? And...

'How did you know my code name?' I asked aloud.

'The letter sent to you a few days ago had the **WRONG** information from the Nuclear Waste Plant... the company we also work for,' replied the Enderman.

Mind blown

'So, you're not **EVIL MOBS** trying to stop me from delivering this package and saving the Overworld?' I gasped.

'Uh... saving the Overworld?' asked the Enderman.

'That's right! We're on the same team! Now, can you stop running away from us and let us explain what's going on?' yelled the Blaze. It was definitely getting warmer...

'Calm down, Flameo. We don't want to burn the kid to a crisp. 111, why don't you come into the house and we can clear this all up for you?' said the Enderman. He held open the door and gestured for me to come into the house.

I had no other choice... so I **FOLLOWED** him in.

☀ SUNDAY ☀
2:03

'Ah, you must be the Zombie that has been causing all the **HEADACHES** for the Nuclear Waste Plant in the last few days,' said an old Husk from the kitchen.

The owner of the delivery location?!

He pointed to a seat at the table, so I nervously sat. He gave us all a cup of **SWEAT TEA.**

'This is Mr. Daywalker, the owner of this house. The Blaze is Flameo and my name is Noir,' said the Enderman, sitting down next to me.

'What's your name?' asked Flameo.

'I'm Zombie,' I muttered into my tea.

'Well, Zombie, you have caused so much trouble for our team... so much unnecessary flying and running around,' Flameo said, still with a bit of tension in his voice. His chair was on fire at this point.

'He's just a kid, Flameo. Chill,' Noir said. 'But yes, Zombie. You have made our job very tricky. Anyway, let me explain. The first letter that you received from the Nuclear Waste Plant actually had a **MISTAKE** in it. The mob typing the letter accidentally copied and pasted the wrong delivery address,' explained Noir. 'This went into the system, which automatically booked your flight and train tickets and posted them out to you.'

'Our team had the job of intercepting you, to give you the correct delivery address. We tried to tell you before your flight to the Forest Biome but nooooo, you had to run away from us,' sighed Flameo. 'Why'd you do that anyway? Did you think we were trying to **STEAL** the package or something dumb like that?'

I blushed and ducked my head to take another sip of my tea but there was none left. So I just held the empty cup to my face. If only the tea cup was big enough to put over my head. This whole thing was pretty embarrassing.

DING, DONG!

'DR FITZ!' I smiled as the familiar Creeper came in and sat at the table.

'Glad to see the Liquid Nitrogen Inhaler worked back in the diner, Doc,' smiled Flameo.

'Just in time, too! I'm glad to see you finally caught up with 111,' replied Dr. Fitz.

'I'm sorry for causing everyone so much **TROUBLE**,' I whispered. I could feel that I was about to sob very loudly.

'It's alright, Zombie. It was my fault. I should've known you weren't our most experienced deliverer... but I didn't realize until you started to run when that Chicken Jockey threw his cup in a tantrum. Sorry, everyone,' apologized Dr. Fitz.

'Why did you tell me about Redstone Inc.?' I asked quietly.

'I thought you were **117**. He was supposed to collect an extra part for the package he was delivering to Mob Village,' hissed Dr Fitz.

Good thing Dr Fitz had brought his Liquid Nitrogen Inhaler this time.

'Well, we have the kid and the two packages. Why don't we make our way back to **MOB VILLAGE?**' asked Noir.

I just nodded sheepishly.

✸ SUNDAY ✸
5:38

'Oh, Zombie, I'm so glad you are okay!' cried Mom as she ran out the front door of our house towards me.

'Zombie!' shouted Wesley, riding his **CHICKEN** towards me with a huge grin on his face. Mom and Wesley gave me a big hug. I could see Dad come out from behind them, too.

'Francis, I'm so sorry about this. I should've read through the papers properly, mate,' Dr Fitz said to my dad.

'We wouldn't have hired him if we'd realized he was only **THIRTEEN**.'

'These things happen, Doc, don't worry. Thanks for looking after my kid,' Dad replied.

'Well, I think 111 has a special package to deliver to 16 Brains Road, Mob Village,' smiled Noir.

Huh?

'Here, read your new mission letter, 111,' smiled Dr Fitz, as he handed me an envelope.

Dear 111,

Apologies for sending the incorrect delivery address in our first letter.

Please return all three packages safely to:

Francis Zombie
16 Brains Road
Mob Village

Items to be returned include:

- Original package delivered to 11 at 16 Brains Road, Mob Village

- Package retrieved from Redstone Inc.

- Teen Zombie sent on delivery mission.

Thank you for all your hard work. You are now officially relieved of your duties.

Best of luck,

The Delivery Program Manager of the Nuclear Waste Plant.

'Are you serious?' I asked Dr Fitz.

'Afraid so,' he replied with a shrug and a small smile.

I grabbed the two packages out of my backpack and handed them to my dad.

'Thank you, **MR. DELIVERY MOB,**' my dad said as he took the packages from me.

'I know a good secret agent... uh, I mean, delivery mob, doesn't ask what is in the top secret packages he delivers... but, Dad, what's in the packages?' I asked.

'Why don't we find out together?' he said.

The first one he unwrapped was the one that I had gotten from Redstone Inc. It turned out to be a spare part that was very important for Dad's work at the Nuclear Waste Plant. Apparently 117 had dropped the rest of the package off earlier.

'We had Redstone Inc. make this part for us. It will help prevent the Nuclear Waste Plant from blowing up if there is ever a **GLITCH** in a future update,' Dad explained.

'If you hadn't climbed through the vents and stolen it, we would have sorted out the mix up in reception at Redstone Inc.,' growled Flameo. I think he was still upset about the whole thing.

'It's alright, Flameo, this was a learning process for us all,' said Dr Fitz soothingly. But I could see that he was **FLASHING**...

To distract everyone, Dad quickly opened the other package.

'Was this what I asked for last week?' Dad asked Dr Fitz.

'Yup, and now I understand why Zombie was so keen to join the new delivery program and imagined evil mobs were chasing him down,' answered Dr. Fitz, calming down.

Dad showed me what he had unwrapped—it was a **DISC**... for Operation Beta-RAINS 2: Beta Business.

WHOOOAAAAAAH!

'So our son was accidentally sent on a delivery run to another biome for a B-grade movie disc?' Mom asked tightly.

From the look on her face, Dad was going to be in trouble later.

'I was just getting ready for the next movie night,' Dad said sheepishly.

We all laughed... even Mom and Flameo.

'MISSION ACCOMPLISHED,' Dad and I said at the same time and gave each other a high five. But we high-fived a little too hard... both our hands fell off.

Made in the USA
Las Vegas, NV
19 January 2024

84586422R00075